One More Month That Matters

31 Evangelical Essays and Prayers

L. R. Abbott

Copyright © 2015 L.R.Abbott
All rights reserved.
ISBN-10: 1512007625
ISBN-13: 978-1512007626

All Scripture quoted is from the NKJV

Introduction

Welcome to this third book in The Month That Matters series of essays and prayers. If you are familiar with the other volumes, you might find some of these essays have more supporting Scripture references. Please do not be thrown off by this. . . no one is looking over your shoulder to see if you look them all up in your Bible. Nonetheless, when you wonder why I say something, or you feel you could use additional input, then looking up a supporting verse is really the thing to do. On the other hand, should any one essay especially grab you, looking up and linking together all its references could be an enriching endeavor. Let the Lord lead you, and may He bless you however you approach your reading.

You are in my prayers. Thank you for your interest in reading and having <u>One More Month That Matters</u>!

- L. R. Abbott

Table of Contents

Day   **Page**

Day	Title	Page
1	The Impossible Mouth	6
2	Spiritual Lumberjacks	8
3	God's Classroom	10
4	Open Wide	13
5	Maximize It	15
6	More	17
7	Beautiful Baby	19
8	Who's in Charge?	22
9	Take the Dare	24
10	Taking the Cry Out of Crisis	26
11	Milk and Meat	28
12	Faith Escape	30
13	Submarines and Fish	32
14	Perspective	35
15	Two Princes	37
16	Anywhere Church	39

Day		Page
17	A Pudding Without Truth	41
18	Great Moments in History	43
19	Stop the World	45
20	One Little Word	47
21	Intelligence Test	49
22	Go for Growth	51
23	Life Squalls	53
24	What to Do	55
25	Don't Do It!	57
26	Be Aware and Beware	59
27	Be Ready	61
28	Love Lines	63
29	One and Three	65
30	Living Happy	67
31	Book of Books	69

Day 1 **The Impossible Mouth** *Ps. 34:13*

"Keep your tongue from evil and your lips from speaking deceit."

When Wu Ting Fang was minister to the United States from China, he visited Chicago. At a reception a man asked him, "Mr. Wu, I see there is a movement in China to abolish the pigtails you wear. Why do you wear the foolish thing anyhow?" "Well," countered Mr. Wu, "Why do you wear your foolish mustache?" "Oh, that's different," said the Chicago man, "You see, I've an impossible mouth." "I should say you do," retorted Mr. Wu, "judging from your remarks!"

Don't you think Mr. Wu was very gracious in response to the insensitivity shown by his inquirer? I do. That man had his "foot in his mouth" and didn't seem to realize it!

Words do hurt when spoken without consideration of the hearer, or in anger. Like me, you probably need not think long to remember an instance of personal hurt you either issued or received as the result of something said. We need to beware of putting into speech everything that runs through our minds. Some things are just not appropriate to verbalize! We are aware of the childhood rhyme, "sticks and stones may break my bones, but words will never hurt me." It rhymes, but is it true? Words can cut, slice *and* dice a person faster than a kitchen blender. Recently a young girl committed suicide after a peer began a campaign of words which belittled her online and by phone texting. The words we use and what we do with them have consequences.

The Word of God is far from silent about our use of speech. Everyone knows a single match can start a huge forest fire. James 3:15 compares our tongues to that match! That fact should get our attention and provoke us to ask, "What can I do to get and keep my tongue under control?" Thankfully, Scriptures provide an answer.

The first thing we can do is ask the Lord to "set a guard over our mouth; to keep watch over the door of our lips."[1] The one to invite as guard over our mouth is the indwelling Holy Spirit of God. If we ask, He is willing and ready to assist us.[2] With His help the "door" will operate as it should, opening and closing at appropriate times.

The next thing we can do is to "bridle" our tongue.[3] When we find ourselves in situations which we know can bring out the worst in us, a bridled tongue can keep us from failure. Like a wild horse that wants to uncontrollably bolt in exercise of its uninhibited nature, we must keep our tongue's nature under control, or it will run away with us. It will take us in a direction we do not want to go and from where we may have great difficulty to return.

Do you have an "impossible mouth?" Bring it under the Holy Spirit's control and keep it bridled... you will be glad you did.

Lord, help me to control my speech and bridle my tongue. Whenever I say something, I want to please you and bless others.

1) Psalm 141:3
2) Romans 8:26
3) James 1:26

Day 2   **<u>Spiritual Lumberjacks</u>**   *Matt.6:15*

"If you do not forgive men their trespasses, neither will your Father forgive your trespasses."

Anyone who wants to do something of eternal worth for God has had to become very good at forgiveness. This is because to not forgive prevents our spiritual service from moving matters of life to where they need to go if God is to be glorified. It is not unlike the problem lumberjacks have sometimes faced. Lumberjacks cut down trees in one location, then set them in the water to be floated from where they are so they can get where they need to go. However, when the logs become interlocked with one another a jam is created, forward progress is prevented. Then someone must step up and take a risk. Someone must take responsibility, venture out on the logs and free things up. This will get the logs moving again. This is not unlike the "spiritual log jam" unforgiveness creates. . . A marriage is in danger of dissolve and the situation is held in place with no movement toward resolve. This makes for a spiritual log jam. A young believer is anxious to see answered prayer, but harbors resentment towards someone who has hurt them – there is a log jam. A woman cannot commit to a trustworthy man because of other faces still etched on her soul – one more log jam. In each of these cases and a myriad of other possibilities, there is a choice to be made. The right choice can change the spiritual order of things, can unlock an unfortunate state of affairs. The choice to make, the one that will loosen a spiritual log jam, is to forgive.[1] Unlocking such log jams is a hard, risky business, but it is the way to make spiritual progress, to get matters of life moving and bring glory to God.

Speaking of God's glory! He dealt with the greatest of all log jams. Once and for all He cleared the way for forgiveness to flow unimpeded to everyone who would repent, confess their sins and believe in His son's substitutional sacrifice.[2] Because we who believe have been forgiven so much, we are to forgive others. To do so is the only way to unlock the "spiritual log jams" which are bound to happen.

What do you say? How about we become the "spiritual lumberjacks" God desires!

Lord, thank you for leading the way in demonstrating forgiveness. Help me freely love and forgive others the way you want me to.

1) Matthew 6:14

2) John 3:16

Day 3 **God's Classroom** Ps. 24:1

*"The earth is the LORD'S, and all its fullness,
the world and those who dwell therein."*

To equip students for life, teachers use a variety of tools. Any one classroom may have books, maps, pictures, chalk or dry erase board and a teacher's pointer. Teachers use these to help students hear, see and understand what they want to communicate. The greatest teacher is God. His classroom is the world and He too has a variety of means with which to teach us, His students, the valuable things He wants us to know.

God uses books in His classroom. . . 66 of them. They are the books of the Old and New Testament in the Bible. These form "God's Encyclopedia" to which we must regularly refer if we are to learn our lessons well.

God uses maps in His classroom. He has a big one of the world He is reaching out to with the good news of eternal life.[1] It is quite a detailed map because His strategy is to reach every "tribe and tongue and people and nation."[2] Because He loves the world, God wants His students to have a working knowledge of it. Some He even expects to travel it so they can teach His classes by extending themselves to others.[3] Another map in His classroom is of Israel and its neighbors. Throughout world history Israel has been a focal point of current events, so God is always returning His students attention to that map.

God also uses pictures in His classroom. For instance, He holds one up of Jonah and teaches how foolish it is for any person to think they can go where God can't see them. He holds one up of Noah and illustrates the importance of faithfulness and completing difficult tasks. He uses another of Jesus, bleeding and hanging on a cross. As students fix their eyes on this image, He encourages them to consider the necessity of salvation. This extensive "pictorial people library" of these and other historical figures is a very effective teaching tool.

God does have a dry erase board in His classroom. On it He keeps records of all His students.[4] Those who trust in themselves and despise His love and goodness are doomed to miss graduation.[5] However, if their attitude improves and they embrace His kindness towards them, He is happy to change their record and graduate them.[6]

God has a dual-purpose pointer for use in His classroom. On the one hand He uses it to direct student attention towards something He wants them to look at. For instance, He may point to the stars and say, "Look at my power by seeing what I created. I have a name I call each one of these stars![7] What does that say about Me?" The other practical use of His dual pointer has to do with His interactive teaching style. Dozing off by a student, or a dull response to a question He asks, can get them a rap on the head from the teacher's pointer. This is to wake them up and return their attention to what they need to learn for their own good and growth.[8]

So long as we are in the world, we are students in God's classroom. There are no dropouts. However, one day school will be out, its doors will be closed.[9] Let's learn God's lessons while we can. . . let's prepare for the close of school.[10]

Lord, I want to prepare for my future together with you...
teach me the things I need to know and do.

1) John 3:16

2) Revelation 5:9

3) Matthew 28:19,20

4) Ephesians 4:3

5) Revelation 3:5

6) Titus 3:4-7

7) Psalm 147:4

8) Hebrews 12:6

9) 2 Peter 3:10

10) Matthew 24:44

Day 4 **<u>Open Wide</u>** *Ps. 47:6*

"Sing praises to God, sing praises!
Sing praises to our King, sing praises!"

Some people consider themselves singers, others do not. Regardless of how we see ourselves, so far as the Word of God is concerned, we are to all sing. The issue is not that some are better singers than others. The issue is, since God has given us all something to sing about, He desires to hear each of us in the form of song. He is more concerned that He hear our voice, then with the quality of our singing. Perhaps this is why he included in Scripture the words, "Make a joyful *noise* unto the LORD."[1] Anyone of us can at least do that!

Singing gets God's attention. He inhabits, "sits down," with people when they sing His praises.[2] Singing also lifts our spirits, as when Paul and Silas sang while shackled together in prison.[3] Also, our song gives God pleasure, as did David's and others when they transported the ark of covenant to Jerusalem.[4] What about King Jehoshaphat's singers?[5] They were appointed to sing truths about God's holiness and mercies. This is not unlike the appointment we have received today from one greater than Jehoshaphat!

You are singing – aren't you? If you are not, you ought to be. As Christians we are to follow our Lord's example. On the night of his betrayal, after the Passover supper with His disciples, Jesus sang.[6] This is not surprising, since Zephaniah 3:17 says He has a history of doing this before.

Since our Savior sang, how can we do less than offer the praise of our lips and – *sing!*

*Lord, I offer my voice of song humbly to you.
Help me to open my mouth wide
and give you praise.*

1) Psalm 100:1
2) Psalm 22:3
3) Acts 6:25
4) 1 Samuel 18:6
5) 2 Chronicles 20:21
6) Matthew 26:30

Day 5 **Maximize It** Psalm 33:6

"By the word of the LORD the heavens were made,

and all the host of them by the breath of His mouth."

It is a great error to minimize the power of the Word of God. The Greek word translated "power" in the New Testament is "dunamis"- the same word from which we get our English word "dynamite." The explosive power of whatever God says is why He can confidently say, "My word shall not return to me void, but it shall accomplish that which I please."[1] Christ demonstrated this power when His words calmed a violent storm,[2] made the blind to see,[3] or raised a dead man back to life.[4] When on display this power is able to change a man and the course of history.

Consider when King Josiah discovered the Word of God had been neglected and not given the attention it deserved. He brought it before all his people so they could make changes and conform to God's will. By doing so he averted a national disaster and ushered in a time of reform and blessing.[5] Even when Christ was crucified, unable to gesture with his hands, too exhausted to speak many words; even then, the few words He did speak had powerful impact. For instance, because He who *never* sinned said, "Father, forgive them, they do not know what they are doing," we who *have* sinned recognize our need to forgive others. Or, when He said, "It is finished!" we acknowledge it as a rallying cry that heralds salvation by grace through faith in His completed work. The power of those three words have brought peace and rest to multitudes of believers. That's power! Let's not forget too, the words publicly displayed above Christ's head on the cross, "Jesus of Nazareth, the King of the

Jews."[6] This sign has been called "the first gospel tract" and multitudes of people have pondered its message more than any road- side neon sign ever seen. Now that is what I call power!

Dear child of God, do not minimize the power of God's Word. Why, one verse, John 3:16, may be responsible for more people entering the Kingdom of Heaven than all Scriptures combined. This verse has been called "the gospel in a nutshell" because of its brevity and content. God's good news is all there, everything anyone needs to be saved. If we had only this one verse, but not the rest of God's Word, we would have so much!

Rather than minimize the power of God's Word, let's maximize it. Like King Josiah, we can start by giving it the attention it deserves.

Lord, thank you for your wonderful Word.

Help me to maximize its power by giving it priority in my life.

1) Isaiah 55:11
2) Mark 4:39
3) Mark 10:52
4) John 11:43, 44
5) 2 Chronicles 34:14-33
6) John 19:19

Day 6   **More**   Lk. 12:15

"One's life does not consist in the abundance of things he possesses."

A man rich in finances was asked how much money was enough. His answer? "Just a little bit *more*." That was always his answer.

More... *More* is an epidemic problem among humans. Their quest for *more* leaves them well short of experiencing where real life is found. Scripture declares, "A man's life does not consist in the abundance of things he possesses."[1] God has made it clear, real life is not achieved in the procuring of *more* and *more* things. In fact He says, "What will it profit a man if he gains the whole world, and loses his own soul?"[2] Excuse me, but isn't that to say a person could have it all– cars, boats, houses, lands, servants, money - you name it, and they would still come up wanting? Wanting what? They've got it all! Oh, I see... still wanting... wanting *more*.

Is *more* some kind of incurable disease? Perhaps. After all, it can certainly produce symptoms like depression, high blood pressure, workaholism, and nervousness. Whatever else it is, for those who aspire to it, *more* is a life sucking spiritual leech, a parasite that must die if the host is to truly live.[3]

So, if life does not consist in the abundance of things a person possesses... if the answer to real living is not in acquiring *more*, what is the alternative? It is contentment, present contentment with what one has.[4] The apostle Paul wisely says, "Be content with what you have."[5] In that same verse he also warns against covetousness, wanting what others have. Acquiring a healthy measure of contentedness will yank that spiritual parasite *"more"* right off us and joy and humility will have opportunity to take root in our soul. Being content sure beats being anxious, nervous and worried!

You were not designed by the Creator to bear the parasite of constantly procuring *more*. Why not relax, be satisfied with what you have and know that *Jesus* is all you need.[6]

Lord, help me to be content with what I have.

Thank you that you meet all my needs.

1) Luke 12:15

2) Mark 8:36

3) Colossians 3:5, 6

4) 1 Timothy 6:6

5) Hebrews 13:5

6) Philippians 4:9

Day 7   **Beautiful Baby**   *Prov.30:4b*

"Who has established all the ends of the earth?

What is His name, and what is His Son's name, if you know?"

"Isn't he just perfect!" says many a glowing parent of their newborn baby. "Look at his smooth skin! He has the cutest little fingers and toes! Oh, he looks just his father when he was a baby (sigh)!" Yes, yes, we get it. There is certainly much about newborns that makes us want to "oo" and "ah." Still, the truth of the matter is, that cutie is endowed with a sin nature handed down to him through his parent. Before long, that nature will raise its ugly head and the child will have lost something of its seeming innocence.

There is just one child born of woman whose innocence remained unblemished as He grew and matured into a full man.[1] The "oos" and "ahs" need never end relative to His character and behavior. Though Jesus *was* human, he *was* different in that He never sinned.[2] Imagine it, a man whose earthly life spanned 33 years, yet He never sinned – not even once!

How did he do it? What was his secret? Let's see... perhaps it was his habit of getting up early for his quiet time every day,[3] or was it the extended prayer times He was known to practice?[4] Maybe it was His capacity to quote Scripture in combating temptation.[5] Are one of those things the answer to Christ's purity? I think there is more to it. A better understanding of Christ's sinless life is found when we factor in his virgin birth. He was conceived, not by the seed of a man, but by miracle of the Holy Spirit.[6] The result of this was he did not receive the Adamic, fallen nature all other humans have.[7] As Immanuel, "God with us," he received a body prepared for his coming.[8] His "earth walk" would be the continuation of the sinless life that was his attribute as second person of the trinity in eternity past.[9]

To put the "secret" of Christ being sinless into its briefest context, it may simply be said, "Jesus was God and God cannot be corrupted by sin"... no, not even if God chooses to take on human flesh and live among us for 33 years. True, but true too is the fact He was 100% man as well as 100% God.[10] That he was God, does not lessen what He endured as a sinless man on earth. He was tempted like any man.[11] His own temptation, as well as the sins of people around him, would not be easy for His perfectly pure soul to endure. With that pure soul He went to the cross, shed his blood and gave his life – not for his own sin, but to take away sin for others.[12] He put up with man's ignorant and duplicitous ways for 33 years, then willingly laid down his life to procure *our* eternal salvation, not his own.[13] Because of his love for us[14] he submitted to his Father's will and, as the Good Shepherd, gave his life for his sheep.[15]

We owe the Godman, Jesus Christ, a debt we could never pay.[16] He the holy, righteous, sinless Son of God, "was made sin for us, that we might be made the righteousness of God in Him."[17]

Although He is no longer a baby, let's keep the "oos" and "ahs". going for Jesus Christ – his Father still does.[18]

Lord, I worship you,
the sinless Son of God. Thank you
for your righteous life and victory over sin.

1) Luke 2:40

2) 1 Peter 2:22

3) Mark 1:35

4) Luke 6:12

5) Matthew 4:1-1

6) Luke 1:35

7) Romans 5:18,19

8) Hebrews 10:5

9) Exodus 15:11

10) Romans 8:3

11) Hebrews 4:15

12) Hebrews 12: 3, 4

13) Matthew 26:39

14) 1 John 4:9, 10

15) John 10:11

16) 2 Corinthians 8:9

17) 2 Corinthians 5:21

18) 2 Peter 1:17

Day 8 — Who's in Charge? — Ps. 45:6

"Your throne, O God, is forever and ever."

Pharoah had one, David and Solomon too. They are the property of kings, rulers and authorities who judge arguments, exercise power, and make life and death decisions. The privilege to use them is just for a season, except in the case of one which was established before all others, one that remains permanent and eternal. What am I alluding to? Thrones, that's what. Those fixtures, the seats upon which the movers and shakers of history have and do sit. Yes, we still have them today. Perhaps less elaborate as in bygone years, but they are thrones, nonetheless. Even the President of the United States must sit on something! Like other seats of authority, his power is not inherent to the "throne," the chair, he sits on. Someone else may sit in the empty seat behind the oval office desk, but that person does not come to it with the endued power the people have given only to the president. Similarly, only Christ can bring to his throne the authority and power entrusted to him by his Father.[1]

What exalts the throne of Jesus above all others is that all earthly "throne sitters" are subject to His ultimate authority. This is why earth's kings and authorities are wise to acknowledge, seek, ask advice and respect Him. If they do this, they and their people are better off for it. However, when they exclude God from their thoughts, resent His authority and deny Him, they only to it to the detriment of their nation.

It is a big responsibility to be in charge of a throne. We think of thrones as only for a few entitled, specially chosen people. Actually, each of us has a throne centrally located in our heart. For most people, self sits on their throne, commanding feelings and making choices that effect their own and others' lives. However, some have wisely displaced self[2] and voluntarily given authority over their throne to the King of Glory, Jesus. By vacating their throne, they willingly submit to His Lordship. Why do they do it? They do it because they are convinced, He can successfully bring order to their inner kingdom. They have a confidence and trust in Him which they know they could never put in themselves.[3] They also know that, by yielding their temporary throne to Christ's authority, they will reap the benefits of His eternal throne.[4] Did you know these things? Who sits on your throne?

Lord, you are worthy to sit on the throne of my heart.
Reign over me and make me the person I can be
by your grace and for your glory.

1) Luke 1:32

2) Romans 12:1

3) Jeremiah 17:9

4) Psalm 103:19

Day 9 **<u>Take the Dare</u>** *3 John 11a*

"Beloved, do not imitate what is evil, but what is good."

Have you recently given any thought to God's prophet Daniel? Me either, but this is remedied for me by writing this essay, and for you by reading it. Daniel's good character is worthy of our emulation, but to follow his example we must keep it before us. So, what did the prophet have going for him that would make us want to dare to be like him?

For starters, Daniel had a disciplined prayer life. He faithfully prayed three times a day.[1] He talked to God and God responded by giving him wisdom, protection and courage. As with Daniel, our life includes puzzling circumstances, danger and challenges for which we desperately need God's help. To expect to receive it we must faithfully pray as Daniel did.

Next, Daniel trusted in God's sovereignty.[2] As a person drafted into foreign service by his nation's Babylonian enemies, this belief in God's ruling over the affairs of men kept Daniel out of despair that would have discouraged his faith. Faith does not operate well where despair presides. If we adopt Daniel's good attitude and believe that "all things work together for the glory of God,"[3] we too can overcome and accept with grace whatever challenges we face.

Another desirable trait of Daniel's life was his personal study of God's Word. He did not have the whole Bible as we do now, but what he had he used. As a result, his reading from the book of Ezekiel[4] brought him illumination from God. Illumination is spiritual enlightenment and something we all need. However, we will only receive it if, like Daniel, we spend time in God's Word.

Lastly, Daniel was aware his life was only one part of something greater than himself, part of a spiritual battle[5] to which he, his prayers and his knowledge of Scripture were all tied. Our lives are like that too for, like Daniel, "we do not wrestle against flesh and blood, but against principalities, against powers, against the rulers of darkness of this age, against spiritual hosts of wickedness in the heavenly places."[6]

Let's make a regular effort to remember Daniel, and let's take actions to follow his good example. Let's dare to be like him.

Lord, your servant Daniel is a good example for me to follow.

Help me to be like him, help me to do as he did.

1) Daniel 6:10

2) Daniel 4:25

3) Romans 8:28

4) Daniel 9:2

5) Daniel 10:10-14

6) Ephesians 6:12

Day 10 **<u>Taking the Cry Out of Crisis</u>**   Ps. 109:21

*"But you, O God the Lord, deal with me for
your name's sake; because your mercy is good, deliver me."*

The placing of two written Chinese characters together – one for danger and another for opportunity – is what makes up the Chinese word for "crisis." In English we define "crisis" as a decisive turning point, a time arrived at where an important decision must be made.

Have you experienced a crisis in your life? If not, you have not lived very long.[1] Truth be told, during your earthly pilgrimage you will probably experience more than one time of crisis. When you do, you will be confronted with the prospect of opportunity and danger... opportunity because there is something favorable to be derived from a difficult circumstance you are in, and danger because you may make a wrong choice and squander something good that could have come out of a challenging situation.[2] This seeming "tug of war" associated with our being in difficulty is always uncomfortable. Being made to feel uncomfortable is the reason most of us would prefer to avoid a crisis.

Christians need to step up with faith and courage to any crisis that confronts them.[3] Rather than falling apart and becoming dysfunctional when something happens, we first need to go to God in prayer.[4] Whatever is going on has not taken Him by surprise.[5] He is not shaken by it.[6] Because God is good, He has something good[7] in store for us as we humble ourselves,[8] admit our weakness,[9] and acknowledge His strength,[10] presence[11] and promises.[12] As we do these things, His peace, grace and mercy will become a part of our present experience.[13] This is how we will take advantage of a crisis. This is how we will make the most of an opportunity and grow. To put our faith to work in a crisis and trust God is the right choice. This is how we can build our faith up and glorify Him.[14]

> *Lord, I know that sooner or later a crisis will confront me.*
> *Prepare me to use it as an opportunity to grow spiritually*
> *so, I can glorify you.*

1) James 1:2, 3

2) 1 Peter 1:7

3) Joshua 1:9

4) Philippians 4:6

5) Jeremiah 29:11

6) Psalm 18:2

7) Psalm 25:8

8) James 4:10

9) Psalm 6:2

10) Psalm 89:8

11) Hebrews 13:5b

12) 2 Peter 1:4

13) Psalm 23

14) Psalm 34:3, 4

Day 11 **Milk and Meat** 2 Peter 3:18

*"Grow in the grace and knowledge
of our Lord and Savior Jesus Christ."*

Christian spiritual development is like the stages of a person's physical development. A physical birth we all have, a spiritual birth we all need.[1] In other words, everyone should have two birthdays... a physical one first, a spiritual one second. When physically born we are endued with the sin nature of our ancestors Adam and Eve. Later, after growing physically, when we are old enough to know what we are doing we can be born spiritually and receive the new nature of our sin bearer, Jesus Christ. Just as our first birth was what gave us the capability to grow physically, so too it is our second birth which gives us the capacity to grow spiritually.[2] In either case, physical or spiritual, the same thing is true... no birth – no growth.

Our sin inherited from Adam was placed upon Christ when He died on the cross and took the punishment we deserved. If we believe this and call on Jesus, believing him to be a risen Savior, God blesses us with forgiveness of sin and gives us our second birthday, a spiritual one. This happened for me at age 23, my sisters in their 30s, my father at 63 and my grandmother at age 83. Although we came to Christ at different physical ages, each of us needed the same spiritual food for nourishment and growth. God provided this food in the form of the "milk" of His Word.[3] No matter our physical age when we came to Christ, not one of us was ready to eat spiritual "meat," no, not any more than we would have been able to eat steak as newborns. We were expected to be satisfied and thrive solely on milk. Milk is what God provides through His Word to those who have received new spiritual life. It is those things easy and nourishing to digest. This makes sense. It takes time to mature before a baby can be expected to be able to chew and eat meat. The same is true spiritually. Spiritual meat are those things more difficult to understand.[4] Understanding them necessitates having previously received a healthy balance of spiritual milk. Until a person has had this, the spiritual meat of God's Word must wait. Then, after they have grown up some, they will be able to properly "chew" and digest the things more difficult to understand.

To cooperate with God in your spiritual maturing, do not ignore digesting sufficient amounts of the "milk" of His Word. Without it you will never grow teeth strong enough to chew and digest the "meat" God wants to offer you.

Lord, thank you for the milk of your Word and the nourishment it provides. Help me cooperate with you in my maturing so I can enjoy the meat you have for me.

1) John 3:7   2) 2 Cor. 5:21   3) 1 Peter 2:2

4) 1 Corinthians 3:2

Day 12 **Faith Escape** Acts 26:28

"Agrippa said to Paul,

`You almost persuade me to become a Christian."

Unlike us, God is pure, with no blemish or fault, without sin. [1] This is how He always has been and how He always will be.[2] It is the reason we say He is "holy."[3] It is why around His throne angels unceasingly proclaim Him as "Holy, Holy, Holy!"[4]

What can be heralded about God cannot be said of us.[5] As inheritors of a fallen nature, we consistently fall short of God's glory.[6] Distanced from Him as we naturally are,[7] we must seek reconciliation[8] with Him in order to enjoy His fellowship.[9] Fortunately, He has provided the way for us to have a relationship with Him through faith in His son.[10] It is our acceptance of Christ which removes the estrangement[11] from God that was our previous dilemma due to unbelief.[12] Sadly, those who do not take advantage of this "faith escape" remain stranded and distant, separated forever from their creator.[13] This is not an appealing prospect in which to enter death![14] When endangered by fire, any apartment dweller would be wise to use an available fire escape. The alternative is to seal one's fate by remaining trapped in a burning building. Very unwise!

Festus and Agrippa were Roman officials who unwisely refused to take God's way to safety. The apostle Paul pointed to God's "faith escape" when he testified to these officials of his own conversion and Christ's death, burial and resurrection. Unfortunately, Festus dismissed Paul as "crazy"[15] and Agrippa adopted a superior attitude to allude Paul's question.[16] Both men preferred to stay in a burning building rather than make an honest assessment of Paul's claims. Many people today make the same mistake Festus and Agrippa did. By so doing, they remain distanced from God, unconverted, the objects of God's wrath[17] rather than His mercy.[18] Because they refuse to take the "faith escape" they remain in their sins, and their creator, who is "Holy, Holy, Holy," has no recourse but to judge them as unworthy to enter His heavenly kingdom.[19]

If you have taken the "faith escape," thank God you did and point others in its direction. . . everyone is not like Festus and Agrippa.

Lord, thank you for making faith in your Son the way to escape your wrath. Help me point others to this truth.

1) 1 John 1:5
2) Malachi 3:6
3) Leviticus 21:8b
4) Revelation 4:8
5) 1 Samuel 2:2
6) Romans 3:23
7) Psalm 51:5
8) 2 Corinthians 5:20b
9) 1 John 1:3
10) John 3:16
11) Isaiah 59:2
12) Romans 10:14a
13) Genesis 1:27
14) Matthew 13:49, 50
15) Acts 26:24
16) Acts 26:27, 28
17) John 3:18
18) Proverbs 28:13
19) John 3:3

Day 13   **Submarines and Fish**   John 3:30

"He must increase, but I must decrease."

Nothing nips at a Christ follower's heels so much as temptation. The tendency to cross the line and enter into "no man's land," the area between a thought and acting on it, is so alluring that we often quickly find ourselves on the opposing side, surrendered to sin before having given up much of a fight. This results in our experiencing conviction, confession, and a need to repent. Our heavenly Father, as He follows us through these responses, graciously provides the forgiveness, cleansing and restoration we need so we can maintain our fellowship with Him.

The challenge to maintain vigilance in the war to preserve personal purity ratchets up a notch when a person falls repeatedly to the same temptation. It is this that led the apostle Paul to proclaim, "O wretched man that I am! Who will deliver me from this body of death? I thank God – through Jesus Christ my Lord."[1] To experience victory over temptations we do well to personally identify with Paul's emotional outburst. We must understand we are no less wretched,[2] no less in need of deliverance,[3] no less in a body of death,[4] no less in need to be grateful,[5] and no less in need of the Savior[6] than Paul was. He knew that dependence on Christ can deliver us from temptation now[7] and from the very presence of sin later.[8] The question to ask ourselves today is, "What can I do to experience less capitulation to temptation and more victory over sin?" One answer to this can be illustrated by comparing submarines and fish.

Submarines have always been a fascination to me. I was able to board one once and have a look around. What I remember best are the cramped quarters below deck and that everything appeared to be made from metal. The sub's interior walls were heavily constructed to support the vessel's outer surfaces from being crushed by the outside pressure produced from deep submergence in water. In 1960 an atomic powered submarine, the Thresher, sank. Investigation found that extreme pressure had folded its outer surface in on itself like a tin can! Since then, scientists began to ask themselves an interesting question... "How is it that in deep-water thin-skinned fish swim around easily and are unaffected by extreme pressure that would crush a submerged submarine?" On examination, they found fish have a built-in internal pressure that counters the outside water pressure in which they live. Because of this they are free to swim unimpeded in their high-pressure environment.

You and I live in a high-pressure environment of temptation that exerts itself on us and wants to crush us. We must build up sufficient internal pressure to neutralize this outside force. This can be done by realizing more of the life of Christ in us. Through personal spiritual growth the internal pressure which prevents our caving into the outer presence of temptation increases.

Thank God, "Greater is He who is in us than he who is in the world."[9] As we focus upon Christ, and realize his increasing life in us, the high pressure environment in which we live will not be able to crush and sink us.

Lord, increase my capacity to depend on you more and more for victory over temptation. Help me be faithful to do those things that will encourage my spiritual growth.

1) Romans 7:24, 25a

2) Romans 3:10-18

3) Psalm 127:1

4) Romans 7:18

5) Psalm 100:4, 5

6) 1 Corinthians 15:55-57

7) 1 Corinthians 10:13

8) Hebrews 10:12-1

9) 1 John 4:4

Day 14 **<u>Perspective</u>** 2 Tim.3:16a

"All Scripture is given by inspiration of God and is profitable."

The Alps, the Grand Canyon, the Serengetti Plains and Niagara Falls, each is a naturally wonderful sight any person would profit to see and experience. There are other magnificent places, but no one can see them all. Fortunately for you and I, others have made images and descriptions available of these places for us. I suppose pictures and articles in a magazine like the National Geographic have done us much favor in this regard. After all, getting acquainted with the beauty and grandeur of extraordinary places evokes awe in us. This is good. It expands our vision and rattles our souls, shaking us out of the confines of our own daily environment. We are otherwise in danger of adopting a lethargic attitude toward the majestic world we live in, and it would be sad not to capture the grander perspective such wonders afford us.

The uniqueness of the earth is also accentuated by our capacity to look at other planets. Today powerful scientific innovations like the Hubbard Telescope and the Mars Rover are used to do this. The clear pictures of far, faraway places such technology provides, show domains of stark beauty, yet none so diverse and capable of supporting life as our own planet.

The Bible, like a Hubble Telescope or Mars Rover, is the only source for capturing an "out of this world view" of what the earth's history is all about. Although we cannot visit every place in time, we can traverse the historical pages of Holy Scripture. Its content forms pictures in our minds by which we can experience God's dealings with the human race. If we are not careful though, our look through this history can be like a visit to the Grand Canyon. There, if you are standing in one place, you are impressed, but unable to see the whole thing, unable to gauge its size and diversity. What's needed is a fly-over. Flying over the Grand Canyon can provide an appreciation and view unavailable by a "stuck in place" perspective. This is why many visitors to the Grand Canyon opt to include a helicopter flight.

Do you have the "big picture" of what the Bible is all about? You cannot get it by being stuck in one place in the Word, and you certainly cannot get it by ignoring the Old Testament. To take in the grandeur of the Word of God, why not consider doing a "fly-over"?[1] Just be sure that, when you do, you are not trying to do it in a jet plane!

Lord, help me make the effort to spend time in all of your Word. I want to capture the "big picture" about what your dealings with mankind are all about.

1) 1 Timothy 3:16, 17

Day 15   **Two Princes**   Jos.24:15

"Choose for yourselves this day whom you will serve."

No one has ever been better off for having a relationship with the devil. Satan does not want to bless, heal and build people up. His only reason to relate to humans is to steal, kill and destroy.[1] No one is exempt from his devious efforts to influence them and he seeks opportunity to bring trouble to everyone.

Satan is called the "prince of the air"[2] because this evil procurator has a present sphere of jurisdiction as all-encompassing as the realm of breathable air surrounding this earth. It is from there that he works effectively at what he does.[3]

Satan is also called the "prince of demons."[4] This title speaks to the fact he has organized assistants to help him accomplish his plans. Paris? They are there... Africa, Asia, South America, it doesn't matter. If there is air, Satan's cohorts have access. For this reason, he is also called "the prince of this world." His influence in producing godless systems of governance and societies is felt everywhere[5] as he advances his interests by blinding the minds of people to their need of God.[6]

The only way to escape succumbing to Satan's wiles is through a relationship with a more powerful prince. The Lord Jesus Christ *is* that prince. He is the "Prince of Peace"[7] because he reconciles us to God[8] and delivers peace to our souls.[9] He is also called the "Prince of Life"[10] because He is the author of all life[11] and the only one able to give abundant life that, apart from Him, is unattainable.[12] Thanks to who He is and what He can do, the works of the evil prince can be destroyed.[13] This is something Prince Jesus is happy to do, but He only does it for those who trust in Him.[14] What do you want to do? Which prince do you want to follow?[15]

Lord, I am trusting in you.
Please bless me with victories over the devil and his schemes.

1) John 10:10a

2) Ephesians 2:2

3) 1 Peter 5:8

4) Matthew 12:24

5) John 14:30

6) 2 Corinthians 4:4

7) Isaiah 9:6

8) 2 Corinthians 5:19

9) John 14:27

10) Acts 3:15

11) John 1:3,4

12) John 10:10b

13) 1 John 3:8

14) 1 John 5:5

15) John 6:66-68

Day 16 **<u>Anywhere Church</u>** *Psalm 133*

*"Behold, how good and how pleasant it is
for brethren to dwell together in unity."*

Did you see yesterday's news headline? It said... "Church Meeting Culminates in Dramatic Answer to Prayer!" The report said that the Christians at Anywhere Church met the night before to discuss matters of faith and business concerning their congregation. The church members, knowing there was great potential for difficulty and division, had been in much public and private prayer leading up to their assembly. Debate at the meeting was lively, all feelings were aired and evident love permeated the atmosphere. At the conclusion of their time together all attendees circled, held hands and bowed as the pastor led in dedicatory prayer to the head of their church, Jesus Christ, and others followed in prayer afterwards. Only when the room fell silent did one of the elders close their time together. The result of this gathering was reported to be renewed corporate vision and evident solidarity of commitment by the church's members. Truly, God answered the prayers of His children for this event. The Anywhere Church continues to be on target to bring glory to God.

Would that news outlets *did* carry such reports as this! But they *do not,* and we should not expect otherwise of them.[1] The world will not herald the things that bring God glory, neither will it applaud matters of the Christian faith. The world's reporters, newsrooms, editing departments and cameras are interested in other things. Fine for them. The greater neglect is if we believers fail to acknowledge God's goodness in answering prayer.[2] To neglect giving God thanks for our success is paramount to assuring future failure. After all, we may water and plant, but only God can bring the increase.[3] Whether it is success with our church programs, or the growing fruit of the Spirit in our members, let's remember to give God the glory.[4] He expects this from we who are members of Anywhere Church, not from the world.[5]

Lord, with others I want to bring you glory.
Thank you for your churches many successes...
Thank you for answering prayer.

1) 1 Corinthians 2:4

2) Romans 12:3; Proverbs 16:18

3) 1 Corinthians 3:7

4) Philippians 2:3

5) 1 John 2:17; Psalm 140:13a

Day 17 **A Pudding Without Truth** John 1:1-3

*"All things were made through Him,
and without Him nothing was made that was made."*

It's time the science books owned up to the truth about Darwin's evolutionary theory. As the saying goes, "the proof just isn't in the pudding!" Over one hundred years ago Darwin did not have the advantage of scientific discovery we have today. There are now multitudes more fossils available for examination than he ever had, yet there is still no evidence of any transitional creatures found. The conclusion is in – the fossil records do not prove evolution!

Darwin's once acclaimed study of finch birds has also been discredited. As evidence of evolution he had recorded that the beaks of this species of bird changed in size and shape over time. He is right about that, they do. However, more time and study of this than he could give has now shown that these beak changes revert back over time to their previous size and shape. This means it is of no evidence to a new and lasting change as Darwin previously thought. The finch study and other similar hypothesis of Darwin have been proven inaccurate. There is nothing of what he proffered as "evidence" that still remains standing.

Consider too, Darwin did not have the ability to look inside biology's basic building block, the cell. Today, technology lets scientists look inside a cell, and what they see is of dazzling complexity. We now know that a single cell contains an enormous amount of information on DNA strands and the information is incredibly organized! It is like the script programmers use to key in a

41

command so a computer will perform a task. Our cells are doing what they were programmed to do! But programming demands a programmer! Who did this programming is the question we need to ask. You see, scientific progress with honest assessment proves, not evolution, but intelligent design. I know I am not the only one with a head on my shoulders. There are others who believe that God created.[1] Still, there are too many who don't,[2] too many who yet consider the evolutionary chart showing apes morphing into humans is worthy of consideration.[3] It is not. The proof is just not "in the pudding!"[4]

Lord, how wonderfully you have made all your creation!
Please help people to see and believe this truth and give you glory.

1) Genesis 1:1
2) Romans 1:18-21
3) Genesis 1:24-27
4) Romans 1:22,23

Day 18 **<u>Great Moments in History</u>** *1 Kings 18:39*

"When all the people saw it, they fell on their faces; and they said,
The LORD, He is God!
The LORD, He is God!"

The prophets of Baal are jumping about, cutting themselves and calling out to their god. They are entreating him to send down fire from heaven to consume a sacrifice from off an altar they have prepared. They move slower now than when they began, and their voices have weakened. They have been at this all day and are nearing exhaustion. Many people have been watching them, anxious to see if their god can do it... can send down fire from heaven. Apparently, he can't. This is when Elijah, a prophet of the living God, becomes the focus of the crowd's attention. First, he orders construction of another altar and puts a different sacrifice atop it. Next, what he does defies logic. Although fire and water do not mix, Elijah has water repeatedly poured over his altar. He does not stop until the sacrifice and altar are thoroughly drenched and a ground trench around them is full. Then, looking up to heaven, Elijah calmly calls fire down from the sky. Its flame immediately and efficiently consumes not only the sacrifice but the altar as well. When the flames are finished not a lick of water is left and the trench is empty! The crowd's reaction? Not surprisingly, everyone there, "fell on their faces and testified with one voice, 'The LORD, (the God of Elijah) He is God... The LORD, He is God!" *That*, was a great confession *and* a great moment in history.

Another great moment in history is a more recent event. A man of God poured out the water of the Word of God[1] all over the altar of a repentant heart. It was one heart in attendance in the congregation, just one that responded to the speaker's closing invitation. It happened when a young man rose up from his seat, went forward, and the fire fell as he confessed, "The LORD, He is God... The LORD, He is God!"[2]

Lord, you alone are God and worthy of my saying so.

Strengthen me to testify of you before men.

1) Ephesians 5:26

2) Romans 10:9,10

Day 19   **Stop the World!**   *Psalm 116:7*

"Return to your rest, O my soul,
for the LORD has dealt bountifully with you."

People often feel overwhelmed by the activities they choose to engage in. There is nothing wrong with keeping busy except when that is all we do. If we become too busy, we can become cynical, worn out and hard to live with. This is the reason some years ago a book was written entitled <u>Stop the World, I Want to Get Off</u>. The book discussed the frustration felt by people who saw themselves as unable to "slow down." It suggested we must be intentional about taking opportunity to "kick back"... to let the world go round for a while without our involvement with it. Jesus understood this. He even set an example of "kicking back" for us to follow.

Jesus said, "Come to me, all you who labor and are heavy laden, and I will give you rest."[1] He knows we cannot succeed in navigating this world without rest, so He calls us to where we can find it. . . He calls us to come to Him. Come to Him and He provides the rest we need. He did not say, "Go workout at the gym, take a vacation" or, "go lie down for a while." No, He said, "Come to me." This is consistent with His saying to His disciples, "Let's go off to a quiet place and rest a while."[2] He didn't say, "Go off and rest by yourselves for a while." This is still His invitation to us today, to find a quiet place and spend some time with Him. Why does He want this for us? Because He knows better than we do that in our demanding world we need *rest*. He suggests this rest is not sleeping, neither is it putting our feet up after a day's work. That is not what He is talking about.

He is speaking of the spiritual rest that can only come from spending time with *Him*. He is offering to us the deepest kind of rest, rest for our soul, spiritual rest, not physical rest. He provides it by making Himself available to extend down deep inside us where no other kind of rest can reach.

It is sad to think many people sleep soundly, waking up physically refreshed, ready to tackle the activities of their day, yet they have awakened without the deeper rest necessary to successfully navigate the pressures and tensions of daily living. Why is that? It is because they have neglected to rest their soul by spending time with the Lord in a quiet place. We are mistaken to imagine that physical rest refreshes our soul. Physical rest refreshes us physically, but only spiritual rest refreshes us spiritually. I'm not saying we don't need both – we do. But let's align our lives with the will of God and recognize that we cannot do it without coming aside often to rest a while with the Lord in a quiet place. We will not regret doing it and, that way, we will not get to where we want the world to stop so we can get off.

Lord, thank you for inviting me to rest together with you.
Help me plan and spend time with you
in a quiet place during my day.

1) Matthew 11:28

2) Mark 6:31

Day 20   **One Little Word**   Micah 6:8

"What does the LORD require of you...?"

In the big scheme of what the Bible has to say one word can mean a lot. If you or I were asked to choose and prioritize a list of New Testament words we consider most important, it is likely we would place words like faith, love, grace or salvation near its top. However, I can also foresee our completely leaving one important little word that ought to be there off our priority list. Read and ponder the use of the word "let" in the following statements. For each one ask yourself, "What does the little word 'let' contribute to what is said?"

"Let" your light shine before men. Matthew 5:16

"Let" all you do be done in love. 1 Corinthians 16:14

"Let" not your heart be troubled. John 14:1

"Let" no corrupt words come out of your mouth. Ephesians 4:29

"Let" the peace of God rule in you. Colossians 3:15

"Let" the word of Christ dwell in you. Colossians 3:16

"Let" yourself come boldly before God. Hebrews 4:16

"Let" yourself love other people. 1 John 4:7

"Let" yourself be glad and rejoice. Revelation 19:7

Do you see what I see? The little word "let" in these verses bears great weight. Its inclusion is an appeal for us to allow, to choose, to not hinder something that God wants to do in our life. Throughout the New Testament words thought to be more important are often preceded by the little word "let." When they are, we must acknowledge that "let" is what we have to do if the seemingly more important words are to be active in us. How sad if, as in the samples, words like "shine, rejoice, peace, love, dwell," and "boldly" were understood by us, but untranslated into our personal experience. If they are not, it is because we refuse to "let" God have His way with us.

"Lets" all add the little word "let" to our personal lists of important New Testament words. If we want to "love mercy, and walk humbly with our God,"[1] we will each have to do a lot of "letting."

Lord, I do not want to be found fighting against
the good work you want to do in me.
Help me to let you have your way with me.

1) Micah 6:8

Day 21 **Intelligence Test** *Romans 12:1*

*"Present your bodies a living sacrifice,
holy, acceptable to God, which is your reasonable service."*

People like to think they have a little bit of "smarts," a capacity to solve simple problems, to know what to do when some matter of life requires their attention. Most of us like to think of ourselves intelligent enough to figure out how to fight our way out of a paper bag. Well, there are all sorts of tests to determine mental acuity, but I like the one found in Romans 12:1 of the Bible. This verse says it is our "reasonable service" (KJV) to present our bodies as living sacrifices to God. These words "reasonable service" in the Greek literally mean "the thought-out thing to do, the intelligent thing to do." That being said, it is a test of our intelligence whether we will present our bodies to God. To do so is smart. To not do so is… well, let's just be kind and say not so intelligent, but you can probably guess what I am thinking.

Presenting our bodies to God as living sacrifices is something we do once and for all, then daily again and again as necessary. If we were a physically dead sacrifice, the repetitive nature of this act of submitting ourselves to God would not be necessary, but then neither would we be of use to God in this life because we would be dead and gone. No, we must in this matter follow in the footsteps of Paul who said he, "died daily."[1] He did it to insure that his flesh did not get in the way of what God's Spirit wanted him available to do.[2] Intelligent man that Paul!

How about you? Do you pass the Romans 12:1 intelligence test?

You can pass it the same way Paul did, by relying on the mercies of God and actively presenting yourself daily as a living sacrifice to Him.

Not certain you can do it? Not certain you can pass the test of presenting your body as a living sacrifice to God? Maybe you need to go fight your way out of a paper bag in order to gain the confidence that you can!

Lord, thank you for your mercies.
By them help me form the habit of dying daily
and presenting myself as a living sacrifice to you.

1) 1 Corinthians 15:31
2) Galatians 5:17

Day 22 **Go for Growth** Eph. 4:22a, 24a

*"Put off, concerning your former conduct,
the old man... and put on the new man."*

A growing Christian thrives on the Word of God. The Scriptures are their spiritual food, their milk and meat, their bread and water. The Scriptures provide the nourishment required to form a strong, healthy, new person in Christ.[1] As a person grows in their faith, they become a stronger Christian, increasingly more secure in what is forever their unchanged position and standing before God. The longer they grow, the less shaken they are by the trials of life and the quicker they are to trust God despite puzzling circumstances that come their way. Through spiritual growth their life becomes less like a roller coaster ride, more like a cross-country race over level ground. Along with their maturing faith comes the illumination that God has been schooling them, moving them to the next stage of who He wants them to be.

In this life believers are in an ongoing process of spiritual change, of metamorphosis.[2] That is, their heart and mind is evolving, taking on increasing similarity to the heart and mind of Christ. Then, at this physical life's end, they will leave all that was of their "old man" behind[3] and only what is of their transformed "new man" will go forward. This is because all that was of the old man is identified with the first Adam who sinned and fell. His nature in us is characterized by sin and the flesh which is forever fallen. That which moves us forward is what is identified with the second Adam, Jesus Christ. This measure of regeneration within us is what outfits us for Heaven. In this manner God gets us ready to eventually occupy a new, glorious, resurrected body.

Do you see it? Can you envision it? What goes to heaven of saved sinners is acceptable to Heaven only because it is the fruit of Heaven's King. All of Heaven will rejoice with Him as He receives believers and the harvest of His work in us.[4]

Great love and devotion to Christ should be invoked in we who are the focus of God's mercies! Our zeal to yield to what God wants to do in us ought to know no bounds. He does not limit the extent to which we can become like Christ, so neither should we. Do not make the mistake of trying to achieve this continual personal transformation through your own self-effort.[5] Rather, do it by faith and expect to be changed.[6] Trust in God's Word, His grace and his mercy. Keep your eyes on Jesus the "author and finisher" of your faith.[7] He does not disappoint[8] and He always keeps His promises.[9]

Let the transformation continue!

Lord, thank you for coming to save and transform
me into your likeness. Teach me your ways and help
me to not lean on my own understanding.
I want to trust you and your promises.
I want to be changed and become more like you.

1) 2 Corinthians 5:17
2) Romans 12:2
3) Romans 6:6
4) Revelation 5:12,13
5) Romans 9:16
6) 2 Corinthians 3:18
7) Hebrews 12:2
8) John 10:10b
9) 2 Corinthians 1:20

Day 23 **Life Squalls** Psalm 4:8

"I will both lie down in peace, and sleep;
for you alone, O LORD, make me dwell in safety."

In Luke 8:22-25 Jesus peacefully sleeps upon rough seas in stormy conditions. While He is tranquil and able to rest, His disciples are afraid, expecting calamity. Their reaction to what they perceive as a distressing situation is not unlike that of many storm-tossed believers today. Truth be told, if your sea and sky is calm today, there is no guarantee you will not find yourself in a "squall" tomorrow. Squalls are brief, sudden, violent storms that can rock your boat. Death of a loved one, loss of livelihood, or sudden tragedy certainly classify as "life squalls." However, these storms may overtake you, they are at best uncomfortable and, at worst, they are able to rob you of your sense of peace and safety. Knowing storms like this will at sometime overtake you, it is wise to prepare to go through them in a way that pleases the Lord. Increasing your boating skills can help, but not so much as knowing the One who is in charge of both your boat and the squall as well. The Lord Jesus Christ is that man. You should carefully note what He says to you, take it to heart, and then go forward in peace through life's storms.

What was it Jesus said to His disciples before departure on their journey that day? He had said, "Let us go to the other side of the lake." This is the same as His saying, "I am going to the other side of the lake and you are going with me." Christ's words are a revelation of God's will, and whatever God wills He performs. No wind, sea, or storm could have prevented that boats occupants from arriving at

God's appointed destination. If the disciples had understood and believed this, it would have informed their feelings and subdued their fear. Then Christ would not have had to ask them, "Where is your faith?" Christ is pleased when He sees faith at work in us. He knows it is then we are most peaceful.[1]

Similar to Jesus saying, "Let us go to the other side of the lake," are His words in John 14:3, "I go to prepare a place for you, and I will come again and receive you to myself; that where I am, there you may be also." The disciples felt threatened by a squall during the trip across the lake. You may feel threatened sometime before you arrive to the other side where Christ has prepared for you a place. Let knowing the Lord said He will be there with you[3] provoke you to faith rather than fear when you ponder entering that final life squall.

Lord, help me to know you intimately. Prepare me
to respond with faith to the challenges of life and death.

1) John 16:33
2) Hebrews 13:5b
3) John 14:3

Day 24 **<u>What to Do</u>** Rom. 14:19

"Let us pursue the things which make for peace and the things by which one may edify another."

Is too! Is not! Is too! Is not! Sounds like an argument between a couple of children doesn't it? Too often it is the sound of grown-ups and, sadly, sometimes this goes on in churches. Lacking agreement, not seeing eye to eye, drawing different conclusions about some disputable matter, can leave people deadlocked in what, if left unchecked, can become very disagreeable, damaging discord. What shall we label this when it happens? Bad behavior, childishness, immaturity or bad form, whatever we call it, it's not good. Such actions do not reflect the character believers should be capable of. No, they do better when they are more like Christ. When they are, they are less critical, judgmental, self-centered as well as more ready to demonstrate patience, humility and perseverance.[1]

Things to dispute about between Christians is not a new thing. There is no shortage of them. Matters about appearance, diet, entertainment, holy days, conduct and finances are on the short list, but it is not hard to formulate a much longer one. I suppose, if we all wore tough shells to ward off hurt feelings it would help alleviate the dangers such disputing can evoke, but it is not practical to imagine we will acquire these tough shells anytime soon. No, the answer to the problem can be summed up in one word – love. Self-defense at the time of disagreement with someone is not the best defense, but love is. Oh, you say, but it is not about self-defense, it is about defending the Scriptures. Careful now, there is a reason why some things are up for dispute. Surely there are many clear matters of salvation that are not up for debate. To those basics all genuine believers should adhere and agree. However, there are a lot of other matters each believer may conclude before God according to the dictates of their own conscience. Remember too, believers are all in a process of growth and at various ages of spiritual experience. In a few years they might view differently the debatable thing about which they have a convinced opinion today. What must be remembered is that God has accepted them, along with their present ideas, because of their faith in Christ. We too should permit them to have their opinion.[2] After all, people naturally feel we have rejected them when we reject what they think.

    Do you want to give someone the feeling you reject them because they might see some debatable thing different then you do? I hope not. Show them a little respect and leave them to their own conclusion[2]... besides, who is it to say that you are always right?[3]

Lord, help me to not be a disagreeable person.
My first responsibility is to love others
and always please and reflect you.

1) Galatians 5:22, 23
2) Philippians 2:3
3) Job 11:7-9

Day 25 **Don't Do It!** Prov. 3:7

*"Do not be wise in your own eyes;
fear the LORD and depart from evil."*

Clothes, food and shelter are things we all need. Safe to say too, we all need love, a sense of purpose and some control over our lives. Other people provide for us when we are children, but we take that responsibility upon ourselves when we grow up, then we make our own choices about how we are going to get our needs met. Usually this means finding a job, earning money, perhaps supporting a family. Work is laudable, so long as the it is honorable and accomplished in a responsible manner. Colossians 3:23 says, "Whatsoever you do, do it heartily, as unto the Lord and not to men." We may have an earthly employer who pays us, but our first and last responsibility is to do work that pleases God. Making money by illegal means is not the way to gain His favor. Many who break the law may know about God, even say that they *do* know God, but there is no way their actions can encourage them or others that their words are true.[1] The fact is, their ill-gotten gain is contrary to God's will and they are "short-circuiting" what God wants to do for them. The way they are going about having their needs met is an affront to Him.[2] He wants to show them He can meet their needs His way. Who are they working for anyway? God or Satan?[3] If they are going to go anywhere with God, a change of mind is in order. They will have to cease activities they are presently engaged in and trust God instead. He has another livelihood for them in accordance with His will. It may be hard for them to transition from doing things their own way to doing things God's way, but God is faithful. He says He is able to supply all their needs according to His riches in Christ Jesus.[4] He has done this for others who work in a manner that pleases Him. He wants to do it for them too.

Do not step out of doing things God's way to get your needs met! If you have done this, have a change of mind about it. Stop! It is just not worth it. You only hurt yourself and others when you do.

Lord, thank you for being on my side
and wanting to meet my needs. I don't want to work
for the devil. Help me find and do work you can approve of.

1) Matthew 12:33
2) Revelation 3:16
3) Matthew 6:24
4) Philippians 4:19

Day 26   **Be Aware and Beware**   *Col. 3:23*

"Whatever you do, do it heartily, as to the Lord and not to men."

God made man in His own image, so no surprise that like Him, man loves to "create" things. We "create" all sorts of things, from artwork to skyscrapers, paper clips to submarines. Often, we pat ourselves on the back for doing it. That is a mistake. In so doing we think more highly of ourselves than we should. This is because our capacity to "create" is completely dependent on the fact that God first created. Although He supplied us the brains and materials that make our accomplishments possible, He too often gets little to no credit for what we achieve. Let a person build a chair with nothing in hand, no wood, no saw, no nails or hammer... nothing, then I'd agree that person would have something to brag about. Find me the artist who paints beautifully without brushes, color palette or canvas and I will be appropriately impressed. Show me the skyscraper built without metal, concrete or power equipment and you will have my rapt attention. It is clear, there is no "creation" by man apart from available materials and the mind man has received by God's design.

Man did not create what he fashions chairs, artwork or skyscrapers from, yet he is quick to think highly of himself for his achievements. Neither did man create his own mind to build a store of knowledge about how to use God created materials to make the things he can envision. But again, who gets the credit when man succeeds at anything? Most of the time men do. They get it and take it without giving glory to God. This is often seen when earthly awards are bestowed on discoverers of scientific knowledge.

It happens this way... something God designed created and knew to exist is discovered by an inquiring, God designed mind, perhaps with a microscope built with God created materials, yet who gets the credit? The scientist does, and usually without any acknowledgement of involvement by God.

It is for reason of man's ignorance of his dependence upon God, that his own works, great or small, are tainted by sin. The truth is, without God we could do nothing. The harder a man pats himself on the back for his achievements, the more he demonstrates false pride in his imagined greatness. The discovery process of what God has created should humble people - not puff them up, but that is not often the way things happen in a fallen world.

If we profess to know God, we need to be careful to give God glory for the works of our hands. Sometimes we *do* see people doing it... like when someone receives an award and gives thanks to God in the ears of an audience, or when an athlete crosses a finish line, then falls on their knees in grateful prayer to God, or perhaps when a successful financier unselfishly gives more and more of his wealth for the Lord's work. Such actions can look and seem out of place to an observing worldly audience, but they are always well received by the Father in heaven.

What do you say? How about you and I give God the glory He deserves for the work of our hands!

Lord, I praise you for giving me a creative mind
and hands to work with materials you provide.
Help me to use them ... not to be vainly puffed up,
but to bring you the glory you deserve.

Day 27 **Be Ready** *Ex. 12:22*

*"You shall take a bunch of hyssop,
dip it in the blood that is in the basin, and strike the lintel and the two doorposts with the blood that is in the basin."*

What would you do if you knew death was planning to visit your home this very night? If you were a Jew in Egypt during the first Passover, you would have known what to do. You would have taken blood from a sacrificial lamb or goat and applied it to the doorposts of your house. Having in this way obediently prepared according to God's prior instruction, His death angel would then have "passed over" visiting your home... the death of a firstborn son would have been avoided. If only the Egyptians had chosen to take the same precaution! They did not, and their households suffered the terrible consequences.

It was the application of the blood that protected people that first Passover night. Any firstborn within the dwelling where the blood was applied was safe and saved. Their salvation had nothing to do with their age, wealth, status or character. Death is no respecter of persons. All are sinners. Salvation that night was solely dependent on the presence of the sacrificial blood. This corresponds exactly to what God had promised ahead of time when He said, "When I see the blood, I will pass over you."[1]

What happened that first Passover night is a clear lesson to us all. God has provided for everyone a Passover lamb, His son, Jesus Christ.[2] When we have faith in His sacrifice, we are applying Christ's blood to our life[3] and we are protected from God's judgment.[4] That first Passover the Israelites applied the blood with hyssop plant.[5] Today we apply it to our hearts and lives by faith.[6]

When God looks at us, He looks for the blood of His son. If He finds it, He smiles upon us because He has found evidence of our faith. Because He does, we are safe, and His wrath passes over us.

Lord, thank you for Christ's blood shed for me.
Thank you that my faith in Him brings me
forgiveness of sin and fellowship with you.

1) Exodus 12:13
2) 1 Corinthians 5:7b
3) 1 John 1:7
4) Colossians 1:13, 14
5) Exodus 12:22
6) Romans 3:25

Day 28 **Love Lines** Psalm 40:5

"Your thoughts toward us cannot be recounted in order;
if I would declare or speak of them,
they are more than can be numbered."

She smiles, her long eyelashes flashing as she meets up with her admirer and says, "Hey there big fella, have you been thinking about me?" He, his tongue hanging out (and with eyes as big as saucers) replies, "Aw Babe, you are all I have been able to think about!" Good lines, but I doubt they were considered for use in the classic film Casa Blanca with Humphrey Bogart and Katherine Hepburn.

God is love,[1] so no surprise His thoughts towards any one of His children are more numerous than the sands of the seashore.[2] He is absolutely "head over heels" about his family members.[3] We know this is true, not only because He never stops thinking about us, but also because He gave up what was most precious to Him, His only son, in order to save us.[4] Still, as He adds to His family, it means an increasingly larger number of thoughts[5] directed towards an increasingly larger number of children. What could possibly occupy all those thoughts of His? In Jeremiah 29:11 He tells us His thoughts for us are of peace and not of evil, to give us an expected end. In other words, He is going to bring us to the desirable conclusion He has for us.[5] I'm all for that! It reminds me of the New Testament verse that says, "He who has begun a good work in you will perform it until the day of Jesus Christ."[6] Our Father God rocks! He is working His plan and He finishes what He starts![7] Considering all the thought God has put into each one of us we know He has put a lot into this. Let's let Him know how much we love and appreciate Him. How can we do it? We can do it by fixing our eyes on Him[8] and telling him what He delights to hear.[9] He enjoys and deserves to hear it from us and, let's face it, it is so good to have a genuine lover of our souls.[10]

Lord, thank you for your thoughts and plans for me.
I love you and appreciate your sacrifice, love, and attention.

1) 1 John 4:16

2) Psalm 137:17-18

3) Ephesians 2:19

4) John 3:16

5) Psalm 139:17, 18

6) Philippians 1:6

7) Hebrews 12:2

8) Revelation 5:12

9) Proverbs 15:8b

10) 1 John 4:9, 10

Day 29 **<u>One and Three</u>** *Gen. 1:26*

"Let Us make man in Our image, according to Our likeness."

Christians are often criticized by people who think we believe in three gods. They do not understand our belief about God the Father, God the Son, and God the Holy Spirit. We do *not,* underline *not,* believe in three gods. We *do*, underline *do*, believe in one God who reveals Himself to be a plural entity. The three – God the Father, God the Son and God the Holy Spirit, always work all together, and always agree together when they do. They are one.

Various illustrations are employed to try to aid people in understanding this important doctrine of the trinity. While none is perfect, I think one stands out from the rest. It is this... in the sun we have a massive, brilliant fireball in the sky. It is too bright to look directly at, yet its light illuminates an otherwise dark world. The heat from it warms the earth and starts seeds sprouting. So, here we have three things which are harmoniously one and inseparable, yet we do distinguish between them. What are they? They are the sun, the light and the warmth. In this illustration the sun compares favorably to God the Father who we cannot directly look upon. The light of the sun compares favorably to Christ, God's son who is the light of the world and makes life possible. The warmth that sprouts seeds hidden in the ground compares favorably to the Holy Spirit who, although we do not see Him, works to warm our hearts towards God and produce fruit in our lives.

Please, do not get me wrong. There is a lot of mystery inherent to a clearer understanding of the trinity. I certainly do not comprehend it, but I do believe in it because I am convinced that the Bible teaches it. Similarly, I believe the Bible when it teaches God created something from nothing.[1] Try to explain that! There is no way I can throw that teaching out just because I do not understand how God's creative work was accomplished. Matters like this I accept by faith. I believe it pleases God when we accept by faith what He teaches in His Word. He knows that we are finite creatures, that even if He was to explain everything to us, we could not understand.[2] We know He is all powerful and can do whatever He chooses... even making something from nothing.[3]

God likes it when we believe what He says about Himself, His will and His ways and, yes, He likes to be trusted – especially when we don't understand.

Lord, show me in your Word wonderful things about yourself, your will and your ways. Help me to believe them even when I don't understand.

1) Hebrews 11:3
2) Romans 11:33
3) Genesis 18:14a

Day 30   **<u>Living Happy</u>**   *Ps. 145:15b*

"Happy are the people whose God is the LORD!"

    That everyone would desire to live a happy life is understandable, I mean, who in their right mind would want to live an unhappy life? No one I know. Nonetheless, happiness is at best a fleeting thing. For instance, today someone, let's call him John, is happy about a new 52-inch television he just brought home. However, tomorrow his air conditioner breaks down. It's 101 degrees outside and he learns it's going to cost him all of next week's pay to get the repair. Now John is not happy. Where did all his happiness go?

    I am not saying that happiness is overrated, but is it reasonable to expect we can always be happy? I don't think so. Life naturally lends itself to our experiencing a wide range of emotions, and they are not all happy ones. Feelings that do not make us happy make us uncomfortable, even sad, but they also serve to inform us regarding our complex natures as human beings. Complex because, even feelings often identified as negative, such as fear, pain, bewilderment or sorrow have a benefit to us. When they force happiness aside it helps us concentrate on their own overriding presence. This happens so emotions like fright can protect us, pain can point us to a problem, sorrow can help us identify with the plight of others, and bewilderment can provoke us to seek and find useful information. Working this way healthy emotions, though sometimes mistakenly deemed undesirable and negative, are actually a blessing. Understanding this is good reason to submit to God's control emotions which disturb our peace, otherwise feelings of fear might lead to paranoia, pain to suicide, sorrow to despondency, or bewilderment to disparagement.

Whatever feelings you have, lift them up to God in prayer.[1] In His wisdom He will direct and redirect them in a healthy manner. Though you will not always be happy when doing this, you will be a more secure and happier person who is less inclined to spiral yourself or someone else out of emotional control.

Regardless of whether you think something that happens to you is desirable or not... submit your feelings to God about it. That is the best way to face your daily life[2] and stay happy.

Lord, guide me in bringing my ever changing emotions under your control. Thank you for caring about what is happening to me and how I feel about it.

1) Philippians 4:6
2) 1 Peter 5:7

Day 31 **Book of Books** 2 Tim. 3:16

*"All Scripture is given by inspiration of God,
and is profitable for doctrine, for reproof,
for correction, for instruction in righteousness."*

The last book of the Bible, Revelation, resolves many matters raised in the first book of the Bible, the book of beginnings, Genesis. In the first book heaven and earth are fallen,[1] in the last book both are replaced with a new, renewed heaven and a new earth.[2] In the first is where the tree of life is guarded.[3] In the last is where the tree of life and a garden city is available.[4] In Genesis we have the first marriage[5] and in Revelation a last marriage, the marriage of the Lamb, Jesus, to His church.[6] In the first, Satan enters and tempts Eve to sin.[7] In the last, Satan exits into the lake of fire.[8] In the first, death has its start.[9] In the last, death has its finish.[10] Babylon, the world system that is against God, presents itself in the first book,[11] then is destroyed in the last.[12] Also, the Redeemer who is promised in Genesis[13] is fully realized and reigning in Revelation.[14]

Is this not a beautiful thing? Matters and issues raised in Genesis are developed throughout the many books of the Bible, then everything comes in for a "one book landing" in the final book of Revelation. What a wonderful book is our Bible! Its writings span over 1500 years with over 40 authors from varied backgrounds like kings, prophets, fishermen, a tax collector and doctor, yet in its entirety it is a cohesive whole with a singular message of salvation through faith in Jesus Christ. We have the Holy Spirit to thank for this. Having used various people at different times and places to do

His writing, He is the Bible's author.[15] This Book breathes, it is alive in a way other books are not.[16] Christ is the living Word[17] and the Bible is His written Word.[18] Read it to be fed.[19] Believe it to be saved.[20] Hide it in your heart to be sanctified.[21] See the world through it and it will light your way,[22] deliver you from trouble,[23] bring you wisdom from on high,[24] quicken you for living,[25] and satisfy your deepest needs.[26]

Someone has rightly said, "This book will keep you from sin, or sin will keep you from this book." Do *not*, I say, do *not* let sin keep you from this book! Your sin is why Jesus came, lived a sinless life and died to save you. Salvation from sin is *good news*, and it is why this book was written. You need to make good use of it!

Lord, thank you for your wonderful Book!
Help me to not neglect becoming increasingly
familiar with its important content.

1) Genesis 1:3
2) Revelation 21:1
3) Genesis 3:24
4) Revelation 22:2
5) Genesis 2:25
6) Revelation 19:7
7) Genesis 3:1
8) Revelation 20:10
9) Genesis 4:8
10) Revelation 20:14
11) Genesis 11:9
12) Revelation 18:21
13) Genesis 3:15
14) Revelation 19:11-13
15) 2 Peter 1:20, 21
16) Hebrews 4:12
17) Revelation 19:13
18) Luke 4:4
19) Matthew 4:4
20) John 5:24
21) Psalm 119:11
22) Psalm 119:105
23) Psalm 17:4
24) James 1:5
25) Psalm 119:25
26) Psalm 19:7-11

Works by L. R. Abbott

ONE MAN'S JOURNEY

What does a Christian life look like? The author offers his own up in example. Not that his life is just like yours, but the spiritual truths God teaches him apply to your journey. Come with him on a pilgrimage reminiscent of the one made by Pilgrim, the main character in John Bunyan's immortal classic <u>Pilgrim's Progress</u>. On the way to the Celestial City, Pilgrim did not avoid every pitfall, and neither did the author. What about you? Have you ever strayed, ever failed to stay on the right path? Confirm you are on the right path. Find strength for your pilgrimage and get to where you want to arrive... read <u>One Man's Journey</u>.

THE MONTH THAT MATTERS SERIES

A MONTH THAT MATTERS
ANOTHER MONTH THAT MATTERS
ONE MORE MONTH THAT MATTERS

If you enjoyed this volume in the Month That Matters series, you will also enjoy the other two books in this set of evangelical essays and prayers written for your heart and mind. Each book presents a unique set of writings, one for each day of the month. None are too long not to be read in one sitting, but none is too short to be shallow. Take yourself out of yourself for a few minutes each day and read more of The Month That Matters series... you will be glad you did.

ABOUT THE AUTHOR

L. R. Abbott's secular studies earned him a B.S. In Sociology with a minor in English. To prepare for teaching Sociology in colleges he attended graduate school at the New School for Social Research in New York City. There, disillusioned with his search for the answer to life's meaning, he quit his studies and became a practitioner and advocate of Transcendental Meditation. Eventually he met Christ and nothing was the same. In the ensuing years his hunger for spiritual knowledge led him to attend, or complete by extension, classes and courses from Moody Bible Institute, Philadelphia College of the Bible, the Central Jersey Bible Institute and Columbia International University. Now retired, he lives in Columbia, South Carolina.

The author may be contacted at OMJAbbott@yahoo.com

Made in the USA
Columbia, SC
06 December 2022